FACEBOOK MARKETING SECRETS

ANTHONY EKANEM

ISBN 978-1-63997-793-2

Contents

Preface

Facebook is undoubtedly one of the biggest internet wonders of the world. It has become so vast that almost all internet users worldwide and countless others know about it or use it regularly. It is for this reason, and many others that internet marketers have jumped on the bandwagon and harnessed its marketing and selling power for their gain.

Big corporations like Coca Cola and Nike make millions of Dollars yearly using Facebook as a marketing tool. However, it is not only the big companies that are harnessing the huge power of Facebook marketing. Many small business owners, website owners, internet marketers, and people who work from home have all discovered how to make money or boost their earnings using Facebook.

In this book, you will learn about social media marketing and Facebook in particular. You will learn a lot about Facebook, Facebook Fan Pages, how to use it for marketing your business and making money online. Do not worry if you do not know how to create a Fan Page or how to use it to market your business. After reading the book to the end, you will be able to create your own money-sucking Facebook Fan Page from the start, and you will be able to harness the great power of Facebook to boost your online income.

Please make sure that you read the book from the beginning to the end. You will discover many Facebook marketing ideas that you can use to make money online.

CHAPTER ONE

What Is Social Media Marketing?

Social media marketing can be divided into two main types. Social networking sites where you can connect with other people as an expert in your niche. You can build your brand, create a customised profile, add 'friends', join or create 'Groups', make comments, send messages, add images and videos, and build links to your website (if you have one). You can publish contents, blog posts, articles, photos, and videos.

There were not many 'social networking' between people on link building websites, and the main attraction of these kinds of websites was quality contents. Also, on a social networking website, you could make a rich, full profile, but in a link building site, you did not have the opportunity to customise your profile.

Today, you can have a Facebook Fan Page, which includes the elements of a "link building" social media website. And you can have as many Facebook Fan Pages as you want, in whatever niche you choose.

Why Facebook?

Facebook was projected to reach over 1.69 billion active users worldwide by the year 2020. On average, at least half of Facebook active users log on to the site daily. The average number of friends a user has is about 200, and even more astonishing fact is that users visit Facebook for over 500 billion minutes per month, according to research. That should answer the question, "Why Facebook?"

Groups or Fan Pages?

Well, this is a no brainer, but it is good to understand the differences because each has its functions. "Groups are useful for organising on a personal level and for small scale interaction around a cause. Pages are suitable for brands, businesses, movies, or celebrities who want to interact with their fans or customers without having them connected to their personal Facebook account.

So, what is a Fan Page?

According to the Facebook Pages Manual (which you can download and use as a guide to set up your Fan Pages), Pages were added to the Facebook environment so that businesses, organisations, bands, and superstars could keep in touch with their fans in "an official and public manner."

For us, the keyword here is "business" because when we use a Fan Page for a niche-specific keyword or product, that is our business. With a tight keyword-focused Facebook Fan Page, you will be indexed fast by the search engines. Your Fan Page will let you be recognised as an expert in your niche, with exposure to thousands of people every day. You can build your list, generate traffic to your blogs or websites, and so much more.

CHAPTER TWO

Search Engine Optimisation

There is no much difference in the methods you can use for search engine optimisation of your Facebook Fan Page than what you would use for your blog or website - anything you want internet users to see and indexed by the search engines.

Below are some things to keep in mind when setting up your Facebook Fan Pages:

1. Every Facebook Fan Page you create should have a firmly focused theme and, if you create several Fan Pages, do not make the mistake of promoting one page on another page. Keep them separate.

2. Make sure you choose a niche that is very active and has many people searching for what you want to promote on your Fan Page. Look for the hot trends in ClickBank, Yahoo, and Amazon, for starters. Search out magazines at your local newsstand; go through the magazines in the niche you are exploring and look for what is selling.

3. Do market research with your favourite market research tool. This is a critical step. If you do not get it right, you will not get the amount of traffic from the search engines that you desire. Take time and give it a lot of thought.

4. Launch Google Keyword Tool and enter your theme keyword. Look for extra keywords you can use that have a lot of searches. In Google or Yahoo, you can type your keywords in quotes to see how much competition there is for pages that use those keywords. Look for keywords with a higher number of monthly searches and a low number of competing websites or blogs. This will make it very easy for you to rank high for those keywords.

5. Once you have chosen your theme keyword and extra keywords you would like to target, use your main keywords in your Fan Page Title and your Profile.

6. Talk about your Fan Page on social media and networking websites. The most popular ones, apart from Facebook, are Linkedin, Friendster, and MySpace. Use Twitter and Foursquare for microblogging. Publish some quality contents on various websites, such as HubPages, Tumblr Squidoo, EzineArticles, and Scribd. Remember always to link back to your Facebook Fan Page.

7. In every profile you create for the different social networking sites, send a link back to your Facebook Fan Page.

8. Every webmaster knows that article marketing is one of the best ways to get blogs and webpages indexed by search engines quickly. They are high authority sites, and search engines love them. Write a lot of articles, and make sure you use the keywords you want to target in the article title, article description, and the content. In the resource box located at the end of your article, send your readers back to your Facebook Fan Page. If you have an opt-in form on your Fan Page that offers a freebie relevant to your article, send your readers there. Not only will you get indexed quickly, but you will also begin to build backlinks to your Fan Page.

9. Some article directories are "no-follow", but that does no matter much because, if your articles are well-written, they will be picked up by other publishers online and published on their blogs, newsletters or websites, thus giving your articles and links a lot of exposure.

10. Visit blogs, websites, and forums that are relevant to your Fan Page niche and post useful and helpful comments, and place a link back to your Facebook Fan Page.

Those are some of the ways you can optimise your Facebook Fan Page. Remember to use your keywords as much as possible and update your Fan Pages often to keep them "new and fresh", and the search engines will love you for it!

CHAPTER THREE

Creating a Money-Making Fan Page

It does not matter whether you already have a Facebook account or not; if you go to www.facebook.com/pages, you will be taken to a page that says "Create a Page". When you land on the "Create a Page" screen, you can start by doing the following:

1. Click on "Choose Brand, Products, or Organization".
2. Fill in "Page Name" (include your main keyword if possible).
3. Click on the box saying you are the official representative.
4. Click "Create Official Page".

If you are not logged in or do not have an account, you will be prompted at this point to either login or create an account. Thereafter, it would be time to start adding contents to your new Facebook Fan Page to make it complete.

The first thing you need to do is to add an image to your Page. Choose an image that represents what your Page is about rather than a picture of yourself.

After you have added your image, you need to edit the thumbnail to make sure that it includes the portion of your image that is most relevant. After you have added your image, hover your cursor on the top right corner of the image. This will open a box with a pencil sign that says, "Change Photo." Click on "Change Photo", and a drop-down box will appear. Click "Edit Thumbnail" and follow the instructions to make necessary adjustments and, after that, click "Save."

There is a small box under the image that asks you to say something about your Page. Make sure to fill this box out. Next, click on the "Info" tab at the top of the page. On this page, you will have two fields to add information to, if you desire. The first field is "Basic Info", and it has a place to insert the date your business was established. The next field is "Detailed Information," so you can explain more about your business.

When you finish with these two sections, click on "Done Editing" and move to the next screen. Under your image, you will see "Edit Page." If you click this, you will be taken to a section where you can customise your Fan Page the way you want to. There are too many options to discuss in detail here. You must explore your options and pick the ones that best meet your needs and the interests of your potential fans. Once you have created your first Facebook Fan Page, it will become progressively easier to create more pages.

Visit the right sidebar and under "Help with Your Page" is a link "For tips and information about Facebook Pages". Click on it, and it will take you to a page that will explain everything to you. There are a *Start Guide* and a Manual that you can download and refer to as you progress.

Here are some tips you should keep in mind:

1. Keep your page title short because when you add contents, your title is added to each post.

2. If you want to, you can choose a "vanity" URL after you have twenty-five fans.

3. The maximum size for a Fan Page image is 200 pixels (width) by 600 pixels (height). Use the full size if possible.

4. Fill out the *About Us* box below your image and include a clickable link back to your main blog, or wherever you choose.

5. Using the Social RSS application, you can bring your blog posts onto your Fan Page.

6. Let your fans also post on your Fan Page so that when someone comes to your page, it will look alive with a lot of interactions.

The above are just a few tips on how to set up your Fan Page. More will be covered throughout the rest of this book.

CHAPTER FOUR

Monetising Your Facebook Fan Page

One of the simplest ways to make money with your Facebook Fan Page is to find a product you want to promote from online marketplaces, such as Amazon and ClickBank. Build your Fan Page around the product. But do not jump to do this! Ensure your Fan Page is up and running before you start trying to "sell" to your Fans.

A good way to do this is first to offer some free contents that are of high quality – something like a mini-course that is related to your chosen niche. Many people opt-in to a mini-course than many other types of free offers. But make sure it is of high quality and relevant to your Fan Page community.

When your fans come to trust your page, and it is popular, you can use a tab to send your Fans to your affiliate sales page directly. Once your fans trust and believe in you, they will be more accepting of the products you recommend to them to meet their wants and needs. It is a no brainer!

Always remember to insert your affiliate link, where appropriate, into any eBook, mini-course, or newsletter that you give to your Facebook Fans for free.

An alternative option is to build a mailing list with your Fan Page. If you create a landing page with "Static FBML" (Facebook Markup Language), you can offer visitors who come to your Fan Page the chance to sign up for your free mini-course, ebook or video for free, without selling anything to them at this time.

Set up your autoresponder with your preferred client, including aweber.com or getresponse.com. Add the "Static FBML" application to your Facebook Fan Page, and follow the simple instructions.

You can also make money from your Facebook Fan Page selling your product or CPA offers. When your fans read about your offers on your Fan Page, they can easily refer their friends too who are more likely to buy whatever you are offering based on their friends' recommendation.

CHAPTER FIVE

Build a Relationship with Your Facebook Fans

One good thing about Facebook Fan Pages is that you can send updates via email to all your fans at the same time. This is not so with your profile page. Therefore, when you have a unique article, or a promotion, or some great information, you can let all your fans know. Just do not spam them!

If you have set up your SEO correctly - putting your keywords in the title and elsewhere on your Fan Page - when people search using your keywords, they will find you. When they land on your page, make sure they find a well-structured, lively Page that gives them more than they expected.

Here are some interesting statistics from Facebook:

1. The average Facebook user has 200 friends.

2. More than 25 billion pieces of contents (web links, news stories, blog posts, notes, photo albums, etc.) are shared every month.

3. Some over 300,000 users helped to translate the site using the translations application.

4. More than 200 million people engage with Facebook on external websites every month.

5. There are over 200 million active users currently accessing Facebook through their mobile devices.

6. People who access Facebook via mobile devices are twice as active as non-mobile users.

7. The average Facebook user is connected to over 60 pages, groups, and events.

8. Facebook users spend over 500 billion minutes per month on the Facebook site and mobile application.

9. There are over 1.5 million entrepreneurs and developers from over 180 countries on Facebook.

   Source: Statistics from the Facebook press office.

CHAPTER SIX

Driving Traffic to Your Fan Page

You can use the Facebook Fan Page App called Fan Appz to set up Top5 Lists, Polls, and Quizzes. There is also a discussion application you can use to ask questions to get a discussion going. You can "promote" these items on your blog or website or other social media site to get more people engaged in the discussion or whatever you have chosen.

Go to Yahoo, for instance, and look at their "Trending Now" list and find some interesting topics to talk about. Bed Bugs was one of the trending topics at the time of writing this chapter of the book. To use this as an example, you could make a Top5 list of where the best (or worst?) places to find bed bugs are. You could take a poll on people's experiences with bed bugs.

You could write a quiz on what to do if you are faced with bed bugs. You could also start a discussion about bed bugs in general. Afterwards, put a comment on your blog or website, and send out tweets to people, telling them about your Top5 List! A lot of Facebook users check out the Top5 lists every day, and if your posts are unique and interesting, you will generate a vast amount of traffic from there.

Your Fans will likely respond, and their friends will see their responses and possibly get involved. They may even become a fan of your page. Keep your Fan Page active, engaging, and interesting. Give your fans something to look forward to frequently.

Another thing you can do is to add a "Welcome" page for first-time visitors to your page. You can set it up the way you want to welcome them. You can point out some features of your Fan Page, explain your niche and what you are trying to achieve and tell them how happy you are that they stopped by. You can set it up in such a way that the next time they visit your Page, the Welcome Page does not appear.

If you know of any other popular marketer who is in the same niche as you, you could search their profile and send friend requests to their friends. Most of them will accept your friend request. When they accept, send them a message thanking them for acceptance and invite them to visit your Fan Page.

If your Fan Page has a decent amount of traffic, you could also do a feature on that popular marketer, letting him or her know you featured them on your Fan Page, and they will likely talk about it on their blog and Fan Page thereby sending their fans and friends to your Fan Page. Just remember to be sincere.

Do not forget to put a Facebook Fan Page badge on your blog if you have one. People can click on it and go straight to your Fan Page. This is a good way to let them know you have a Fan Page on the same topic as your blog.

CHAPTER SEVEN

Driving Traffic from Your Fan Page

There are a lot of ways you can use your Facebook Fan Pages to drive traffic to your blog. By using the Social RSS Application, you can have your blog posts appear on your Fan Page as you publish them. It will show an excerpt of the post with a link that says, 'Read More Stories' and another one that says, 'Subscribe to stories from this page.' Thus, not only do they have to click and go to your blog to read the rest of the blog post, but they also have the option to visit your blog and possibly subscribe to your blog "stories."

Publish updates on your Fan Page that talks free things you are giving away on your blog or a contest you are organising. Provide them with the link to the right page or post on your blog. Offer them a free report or eBook if they go to your website and fill out a poll you are taking. But make sure it is something worthwhile, and on a topic within the niche you are promoting.

Mention that if they go to your blog and buy a product you are selling on both your Fan Page and your blog, there is a special discount or coupon they can avail themselves of if they click over to your blog and order from there instead of the Fan Page. They will appreciate the heads up.

CHAPTER EIGHT

Facebook Applications

There are hundreds of applications you can use on your Facebook Fan Page. Some of them include:

1. **Networked Blogs:**Network your blog with Facebook's huge blogger community.

2. **Sweepstakes:**with this App, you can generate and launch a branded sweepstake within a few minutes. Your Fans simply enter the sweepstakes, and the application picks the winner at random.

3. **Social RSS:**This application lets you add your RSS feed to a tab and your Fan Page wall automatically updates.

4. **Fan Appz:**Great suite of marketing apps for social media to help Facebook Fan Pages connect with, monetise, and grow their number of Fans using Top5Lists, Promotions, Quizzes, Polls, and virtual gifts, among other things.

5. **Social Tweet:**This application lets you tweet directly from Facebook.

6. **Show and Sell:**Set up a visual mini-store.

7. **Promotions:**This application lets you offer special promotions to your fans.

8. **Discussion Boards:**This allows you to start a discussion and see where it takes you. This can be used as a forum for your fans.

9. **Notes:**This allows you to write notes back and forth with your fans.

10. **Photos:**This application is excellent for putting images or photo albums on your fan page and giving it more visual appeal.

11. **Videos:**Videos are crucial now. This application enables you to add videos on your Fan Page.

12. **Events:**schedule special events for your fans to attend

13. **Surveys:**Take surveys to learn more about your fans

14. **Coupon:**Special offers and coupons for your fans

15. **My Fan Site:**This lets you use custom HTML and CSS to design a landing page for your fans

16. **Mobile:**This allows you to view the contents your fans upload using Facebook Mobile. It gives you a phone book view of your fans and enables you to subscribe to their mobile contents.

So, go through the list and read the descriptions and pick the ones most applicable to your niche and your fans.

CHAPTER NINE

Conclusion

The whole concept of Facebook Fan Pages is immense, as is the subject of "Social Networking," which is growing by leaps and bounds. What is covered in this book is just the tip of the iceberg, and there are new developments and things to learn each day.

Facebook Fan Pages are a "must-have" for every business or online marketer who is serious about nurturing their community and making money online at the same time. It will be worth your time to check it out.